I0459640

PRIZE WHEEL

PRIZE WHEEL

COLLEEN MICHAELS

Copyright © 2022 by Colleen Michaels

Cover Design: M.P. Carver

Cover Image by permission of author

Book Design: Erin Dionne

Illustrations: Olivia Malloy

Author Photo: Rebekah Sommer

All rights reserved.

No part of this book may be reproduced in any form or by any electronic or mechanical means, including information storage and retrieval systems, without written permission from the author, except for the use of brief quotations in a book review.

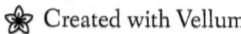 Created with Vellum

It is deeply satisfying to win a prize in front of a lot of people.
-E.B. White, *Charlotte's Web*

CONTENTS

BEAT THE HOUSE

HONORABLE MENTION

For the sixth-grade science fair
I decide to grow a spine.
It takes more work than I thought
I have to dig around the house
scavenging from my family
what will become my vertebrae.

From my grandmother's sewing kit
I pocket spools of cotton thread
unraveling until they are clean bones.

While the other fair girls
build shrines to butterflies,
between these bones I sandwich
my father's poker chips
drilling through the center
of each red and white disk –

disks colored like the carnations
some girls will submerge in dyed water
to prove the inevitable blush,
a cross pollination of projects,
until all results are prom-dress pink.

To grow my spine of 24 bones,
I stack from my father on the back
of my mother's mother
string disk to spool with a fine filament.

The prize goes to the butterflies but my spine
hangs straight, suspended from skull,
casting an honorable shadow on the x-rays
my mother, a typist in radiology,
brought home for support.

FRIED DOUGH TRAILER

At fall festivals, the apple-faced boys
court the fried dough trailer
setting elbows on the counter
with fisted dollars and thumbprint eyes
caught in the dough, immovable
against the thin boys and farm girls emerging,
flustering like maples in this season.

And the majorettes refuse to wear their coats.
Their oily faces are tinderbox for small towns
a bullhorn trills in each breath.
Spinning and twirling, they retreat
from their minders and skip church,
dusting sweet sugar and cinnamon
as they race to keep time.

The mothers claim the sidewalk and guard their town parade
a barricade of folding chairs, fortified by fleece vests.
The seasons have been known to sneak up on them
they won't be fooled by fried dough or false summer.
As for this sweetened makeshift stand,
a sampling, a taste, is enough they will say.

HUNGER IS A SUIT LIKE FARRAH'S

My first job in a sandwich shop
the saloon doors plastered
with the two halves of Farrah.
Red swimsuit, a Mexican blanket,
those nipples. I'd bust through
her and place the orders for veal parmigiana
Large American hots or no hots
pepper and egg on Friday, the Catholic
owner's specialty. He'd make each sub
handing it out, holding back Farrah's
shoulder. Each night the aluminum
stock pot of sausages was put under foil
the top oily, red and dark, a good
burn worked into the sauce.
I could put an Italian to bed, the soft
padding of the roll, a pillow of white
bread, sheets of mortadella and salami
rose medallions of marbled fat
three slices each, angels themselves,
then good provolone, that barely wants to
bend. I'd tuck in tomatoes and pickles,
next oil, a sprinkle of salt and pepper
already mixed together. If you had done it right
it wouldn't want to close.

IN PRAISE OF SWIMMING AT NIGHT

Praise Old Orchard Beach and swimming at night.
Praise the draw of mussel beds to pylons,
the boardwalk, slippery and sharp scaffolding.
Praise the dance club at the end of the pier.
The DJ. *Groove is in the Heart.* The Beastie Boys.
Praise the underside, the B-side.
Praise college roommates and their brothers,
the lifeguards, in orange board shorts,
who stay in Saco, Maine rentals all summer.
Praise aimlessness as brown wide shoulders.
Praise the Sex on the Beach,
the Fuzzy Navel, the Absolute.
Praise the temporary tattoo of skull
and bones I got in the afternoon.
Praise my black bra strap and wet wife beater.
Praise the bad idea to go swimming
at midnight, high tide. Hallelujah buoyancy.

Above all praise my one love,
an excellent swimmer, who hates
The Beastie Boys, and sickly-sweet shots,
but somehow loves me.
Praise navigator, cartographer,
the one who finds shipwrecks.

BLUEBERRY DONUTS

On Saturday mornings, our parents would send us on impossible missions. *Take your sister and go get blueberry donuts. My pocketbook is on the back of the chair*, my mother would yell from the bedroom. They wanted to shut us off for a while, and the blueberry would buy time. More glamorous than a French cruller, you couldn't get it at Dunkin' or across the street at Patty's, where the black and white frappes were cold in summer, the coffee hot at the window, the jelly sticks messy. I'd make my sister find her shoes, and we'd walk down Cedar Street. Past the Sons of Italy parking lot. Past the house of the girl I once made pee her pants. Past the houses where holidays hung out of season -plastic eggs in the trees, hearts taped to windows. Past the park where I would later be felt up by Paul Figgolini both of us in corduroy jackets with loud zippers.

To get these blueberry donuts, we had to walk the tracks and cross the trestle. Looking down into the thick Charles River I could count the suicides of shopping carts just below the surface. Once we found a head bobbing close to the bank. She was from the beauty school and still pretty - her lipstick permanent, her hair like a rich girl, her plastic shoulders forcing her above the muck. We'd pull switches from branches and start whip fights on the trestle. My sister younger, but tougher. My legs like Jesus at the stations. I'd remind her of that head when I needed to. Tell her I'd place it in her dreams, eyes open, put it right next to her pillow, and she'd offer up her whip to the river.

To get to the blueberry donuts, we had to walk past Ming Garden where everyone knew they wouldn't get carded if they ordered enough food. Past the body shop guys with the bad teeth sitting outside, swiveling in office chairs, making double time. Past the glass and mirror shop where we could see how others might see us from angles we didn't get at home.

We could never get the blueberry donuts, knew they were a fool's errand, a gamble. They had always sold out or hadn't been made that day, some story we'd always swallow. The harsh fluorescent lights the only thing keeping the hard dough warm. A trick. We'd wait while the baker put down his hand of cards, stepped away from the Friday night flush. *Tell your father he owes me his paycheck,* he'd say, laughing and serious all at once as he filled the waxy bag with enough sugar to keep us in the game.

IT IS ELIZABETH BISHOP'S FISH

who instructs me to gut
the image of long-line fishing
I had wanted so badly to drop
into a poem about my mother
- not a tremendous poem at all -
but I wanted to pull taut this
line between mother and child
tie us on *one long elegant line,*
I wrote. That was the victory.
But the poem hadn't struggled at all -
an easy catch on the Bering Sea
tangled in miles of violent lines.
Cut it loose, Bishop
whispers from her boat.
This greedy connotation
of hook and drag.
The slitting of a leatherback's
throat is in that line.
And what of the albatross
who dives down famished?
All that neck pain and cursing
now caught in the net.
Mothers and daughters are all
capable of cutting so badly.
Anyone can hack at something.
But to cut clean, to fillet
the fine boned, or better,
to catch and release, demands
clear accuracy.

Let it catch the light
before it goes down, this first poem.

If you must make a fish into a mother,
listen to her shallow breath in your labor.
Cast further, for the venerable and battered

youth of polio and iron lung cages.
Find a use for those mentioned
flies, the greenheads,
who would bombard
you both in pregnancy.
Articulate iridescence.
Long-line fishing – skill less of course
not even fishing -swindles
sharks for their teeth.
They drop to the floor,
eaten alive by lesser prey.
Your mother has bite.
How dare you not stare?
The fishing champion tsks from her craft.
Note the arc above
her dead-eye stare,
her bleached centipede scar,
a sunning, still predator
on her bad leg.
The strain of straps on the pink
two piece, edges ruffled like a carnation,
the one she wore
swimming on Cape Cod
when first pregnant with you.

WHEN ALL IT TOOK WAS MUSTARD

In the photo, I'm wearing a hat built to go over my face
with tinted green circles in place of my eyes.
Thrifty, this combo of hat and sunglasses.
A two-piece. Propped on a concrete seawall,
thin layer of sand, sunbathing on a thinner bath towel.
Thrifty, this family of bologna and Land O'Lakes
white cheese sandwiches. Pepsi cans wrapped in foil.
Through those lenses some strange horizon,
a weird tint of water, sky and ski-lift type ride.
Nantasket Beach and Paragon Park,
my view, my now mirage.

We were a mayonnaise family, still are,
but on beach days my mom would make
us use mustard on sandwiches. We didn't complain
knew it meant we were staying late. Nothing would spoil.
We stayed the day I stepped on the butterfly nut
of my mother's crutch, her own horseshoe crab buried.
We let the salt water, a cure-all, repair the tear between toes.

We stayed through low tide, filling a hole at our spot.
First puddle, then pond, then lake within the sand.
We stayed when it disappeared and we got small and tight,
joined adjoining families at high tide and sang
to the songs of some other family's radio stations.
We stayed through the sunburns, the putting on of tee shirts,
the wearing of towels as turbans and skirts.

We stayed through two packs of cigarettes,
four rides on the carousel, one game
of skee ball (but don't tell your sister).
We stayed until we knew it was certain, not a trick
of tinted glasses, that we would most definitely stop
at Charlie's for fish and chips and stay
until the paper boat was nothing but lost salt,
grease stained in the shape of jellyfish.

GRAND MAL, PALL MALL, PELL-MELL

At six, a baby sister is Cabbage Patch,
a flesh doll to dress in ridiculous hats.
I took her to kindergarten for show-and-tell Friday.
She was okay, but not as good as the Wizard of Oz
snap front shirt I brought in the week before.

The morning of the Grand Mal, the small
doll body of my sister stops breathing.
I am at home hoarding our grandmother while she turns blue.
Our parents at a pancake breakfast are pulled aside by the priest.
I am seized by questions. Could I go to the hospital?
How about the small gift shop? Can I get a cafeteria-grilled muffin?
Once I have learned the word *Phenobarbital,* can clap
out the syllables, I get greedy for a spelling bee.

That week my mom smoked Pall Malls on the apartment porch.
Her hands shaky, she'd gulped in enough air for everyone.
I watched her shoulders go up and down in her leather car coat
looking like she was talking to someone, trying to convince
or ask for a little more time to make the rent.

My sister, now a skier, now a skydiver.
That morning her first trick death.
I remember her seizure story pell-mell,

confuse the ice bed her frail fish bones

were thrown upon with my grandmother's

slip on the slick steps tossing her to paramedics.

This bright white becomes the shock of age

suddenly there in my young father's black hair.

CONFLICT RESOLUTION THROUGH SOUP

When the political poet comes to my school
I make him soup, a vegan miracle
of organic carrots and ancient grains,
and he hugs me. I dodge his appetite
for a third-party debate, labor unions, the sweat shop talk.
My compassion is measured out in kitchen tools;
this soup is brimming with opinion.

My soup shifts shape in the cauldron.
I sagely puree the unsavory and sour
into palatable luxury. Shoe stringed onions
coated in ale and cheddar cling to my spoons.
Third graders unknowingly eat kale at my table.
My soup turns battles into cook-offs, whisking
aggression into bisques and soft broths.

Down to a simmer, I turn the dry cough
of neighbors no longer warm to pot lucks
with my chicken stock and generous doughy elbows.
I slip ginger in the pockets of my enemy
and fill the lean bellies of burglars at night.

For my father I serve something milky
to calm an ulcer from daughters who over salt.
My mother, I give her enough pepper to occupy her tongue.
Now all happily digging for clams.
All floating oyster crackers.

On nights when my love moves to his far side of our bed
his bones no longer against my belly – I serve mulligatawny.
Like silk and fire in the mouth, he comes back to me hungry.

When we are poor and at the end,
I'll take those saffron threads from the cupboard,
drown them deep in an old family stew,
take one last Viking stance in steam.

SLEIGHT OF HAND

GETTING AND SPENDING ON COMMERCIAL STREET

At the Provincetown Library's book sale
our daughter decides to part with her dollar.
There is so much that she could get with it
here, on Commercial Street -
rubber ducks in buckets on stoops,
rainbow beads and unicorn stickers,
all manner of sugar blotting grease.

Since morning this dollar has been gaining value
in her right front pocket. The bill now bullion,
heavy as fudge weighted with walnuts.
It picks up the wet palm momentum that money
always gets – a duty-free frenzy. A sailor on leave.
We steer her away from ships trapped in plastic bottles
talk her down from flips flops that don't fit.

We go to the library, right there in the middle of the street,
close to the headshop and the Lobster Pot.
She heads for the basement, the annual book sale.

Downstairs, it's strong smelling and cool,
like Noxzema on shoulders after a full day of sun.
Her fingers, small crabs at low tide,
walk the spines of the books.

THE PEA DEFENDS ITS POSITION

There are spiders who get
to flush the sweet cheeks
of hungry and idle girls
trussed by pink ribbons.

They are easy prey, palate
content with beige crocks,
weighing down tuffets
until frightened away.

I don't want to work with
hooded girls who haplessly fall
for the ax or fang in drag.
I am no big bad lady killer.

Don't stifle my small power
on fools who cross bridges,
on rubes who start to doze
after a few candied apples,

grabbers of beanstalk, vine
bower, tower length hair.
Consider the smoke and mirrors
to throw one midnight ball.

As applicant to irritate
an insomniac's light slumber,
I worked on the commission
of pleasure. She hired me.

They'll say she was the one to bruise
and I was her green starter for a prince.
Those are just lies, thick mattresses.
She remembers my tender skin like spring.

JURY DUTY, JANUARY

Driving to Lynn District Court
I pass a crib, flush to curb.
On the stoop, a crowded plastic creche.
Shepherds prop each other up like drunk
uncles. Mary in a molded blue gown
leans on the railing, unplugged
her back to slush, waiting to be called up.

IF YOU CAN'T FIND GOD IN THE DETAILS

look for my father, the custodian at Saint Charles Borromeo,

with the congregation for whom he'd blessed the stairs

with rock salt in winter and whose dripping boots

had anointed his floors between pews each spring.

He asked the Monsignor what he could design for God.

He learned the significance of liturgical colors: White for the new.

Purple for passion. Red for the feast of the apostles.

My mother, who worked at a ribbon and paper factory,

brought home odd cuts of silk, small thefts for his decorations.

For every dove, there's a devout bowerbird.

He'd print the Divine Office, the quiet Order of Vespers,

on deckle-edged card stock, making a menu of many courses.

There was the time he, Great Oz of church, dropped a radiator

and dragged it across the choir loft at Tenebrae to stage the sound

of sorrow, the strobe light and rain soundtrack

synched with confessions.

On Easter morning, from the Corona, the gold ring above the altar,

paper butterflies fluttered, dozens of crinolines. Everyone looked up.

Christmas Eve I'd get to dress in blue upholstery with silver threads

and hold my sister, a real baby, in the makeshift manger while

all the beige, coarse shepherds and the flock of hunched third

graders looked on at the pageantry of my family and our indulgences.

MAGICAL THINKING

From my west window I can see
a small slice of a theatre's orange facade,
Le Grand David's Spectacular Magic Company,
above marquee and below sky,
behind the eyelash of winter's tree line.
This juicy horizon vim of sky
pays no mind to rules of sunrise
and saws the day right down the middle.
Conjured by Marco the Magi
each Sunday at the 3:00 matinee,
it tricks me every time
into believing some new
vibrant version of morning.
Due west, wires invisible, no net
where I sit curbside expecting the murals
of jeweled elephants to be ushered
into the crosswalks for applause.

UNMENTIONABLES

Even though her grandmother could thread needles in the dark, the girl would have to read the circular specials to her. So she'd read for fun while eating butter and sugar sandwiches at the kitchen table. If the other grandchildren were over, she'd tuck the paper away. They were already bullies at school like their fathers had been. Like her father had been.

The basement was off limits, but the girl had gotten down there. Had seen the old washing machine and next to it her grandmother's winter clothesline, hung with the stiff, cold shapes of her family. Clipped onto the line were pages ripped from books. The A pages from the dictionary. A child's spelling book. Newspaper clippings of coupons she wanted.

The small girl started to take on small chores, dusting the collection of depression white glass. *I'll let the l lag on my tongue and cut it with the sour k sound. Milk. I'll hiss the end of glass,* she'd whisper while snaking the figurines along the windowsill. Slow winter work.

In the spring they were ready to take the laundry outside. *I'll hold the clothespin bag until your basket of cold tangles is sorted out.* Piecing together the words her grandmother still needed, they filled the line. *A sheet for a sentence. A dishtowel for vowels. We will use unmentionables for silent e.*

HAND TO MOUTH
Invitations and Stationery, Waltham, Massachusetts

The new girl who thinks she owns the tape dispenser is back again. Most fold after a week. Janet from shipping keeps a pool going. She gave this one three days. I saw her talking with the front office girls this morning, the ones who wear black leggings like my daughter does and keep hand cream on their desks. They say the carpet under their desks is filled with static electricity. Poor babies.

Everyone at the work table knows the tape dispenser is mine. I line the invitations faster than anyone. I can even work quickly with the slippery Mylar paper. I've got a system. I put the envelope down, flap up, give it three small pieces of double-stick tape, eyeball the liner, and lay it in neat and straight. If I were a cook, I could bone the shit out of a chicken. I don't need Band-Aids anymore.

Once I did the wedding invitations for Demi Moore and Emilio Estevez. Not many people remember that they were engaged. I keep waiting to see the invites show up on eBay because I know we all snagged one to take home. Sometimes the guys who cut stock will pull aside extra for us. Right now we're working on getting the stock to put together Janet's grandson's first communion cards. We're a team like that.

The new girl keeps asking me annoying questions. I don't *do* questions. *Where do you recommend for lunch?* I don't. Janet and I always bring pasta in Tupperware. Everyone knows that. *Do you think I should suggest handmade paper for a more dramatic effect?* No. I think she should just read what the P.O. says and start taping. And this one I just love, *Do you find the language on most wedding invitations to be more traditional or contemporary?* Do I find? I find that when I'm paid by the piece, I don't have time to think about questions. I wish she would just listen to her music with headphones like the other new girls who don't last.

STINK EYE, IN THE VOICE OF A TABLECLOTH

after the painting *Family Wrangle at Picnic Place - Rain Shower
Approaching* by Quinton Oliver Jones (1969)

Understand that I am theirs. Of them.
We are only showing you the wink,
a telephone game of soup cans tied.

No, you don't need to see the cans.
You know the game. Taste those bits
of tomato in the cold meatloaf sandwich?

That's ours. Not yours. I expect
you've got your own shifty-eyed cousin
and downcast mother. No, you can't

borrow our corkscrew. It's part of a set.
It belongs to us. And by *Us*, I mean, not you.
You thought I'd betray this tangle of family
because I am as plain and simple as hopscotch?

You know nothing of how I was made,
checkered and dyed and washed out,
more turned than an August pillowcase.

I'm the first to be touched, the last to fold.
Never mind the family gossip on top of me,
just sour grapes in a so-called fancy salad.

There is no picnic without me. I had to be
considered, *dealt with*, before any of this nonsense.
I know they now look like damn fool flies.

Still congregating over chewed ears
right before rain, can't even smell it coming.
No. Nope. You don't comment on the rain,
or the quality of the potato salad.
It is an old family recipe. And it is ours.

MAGGOTS AND MILK

For me it was maggots. For her it's the spill
of milk, a kitchen counter downpour.
In every childhood fear there's a thrill.

If you want to test a 4th-grade girl's will
assign her the garbage can chore.
For me it was maggots. For her cleaning the spill

of bubbling white foam that will instill
a gag over wet paper towels on floors.
In every childhood fear there's a thrill

mine an in-ground lead hole just past the doorsill
inside the wiggle of life. Trash in hand, foot unsure.
It was the spill of maggots. My mother would kill

for me. She scalded water and doused down until
my jelly-toed sandal was safe. She swore
in every childhood fear there's a thrill.

So for my own daughter, I make sure to fill
her glass full with bubbles of milk she abhors.
For me, it's the maggots for her. It's the spill
in every childhood fear. There's a thrill.

EASY MARK

THE MORE WEIGHTED THE PURSE

The more weighted the purse, the more necessary the woman.

When the sisters in a family of this currency die,

they will submit their handbags as evidence

having hooked them on their forearms, these Queen Mothers

of Foxwoods Casino and Ocean State Job Lot,

rested them on the backs of chairs around kitchen tables,

rooted in them – 2-for-1 coupons, a kid's prescription, lucky coins,

receipts tucked in wallets, change and tobacco buried in the bottom

and always the bragging rights as brides and babies

free fall from photos in plastic strips. It's not a money thing.

At the wake of the first of the sister to die,

the purses on the laps of the receiving line are

plumped with tissues and extra prayer cards.

Everyone knew her purse to be light in life,

just a comb and a Saint Anthony medal lost in the lining,

her money found after the wake tucked in baking soda in the fridge.

APRICOTS IN AFGHANISTAN

There ought to be an aircraft emergency card, laminated
instructions for small talkers in cases of ignorance.
I looked for one in the pocket of my aisle seat
when I sat in the last row of a flight next to a fatigued boy.
And I knew I was asking too much of him,
asking him to hold my precious skinny latte.
Still, I asked this soldier to hold as I began to spill.
So what do you do? I mean, over there?   He told me it was cold,
very cold, not the dry heat you'd expect. Just cold, like here.

I took back my paper cup, almost thanking him for his service.
There's a good steak house in the terminal!
I hear the apricots in Afghanistan are great!
I told him I thought it must be funny to be seated
next to a civilian like me, unable to navigate even a cup of coffee.
He said politely *No Ma'am, it's not that funny at all.*

The attendant leaned over me and offered him whatever he wanted:
The big box of M&M's, Pringles, full can of Coke.
Take them, she said. *It's what we do for service members.*
You won't have to pay.
She dumped it all on my tray as the seat-belt light came on.
I was overflowing with small concessions.

RESCUES

The Charles River bass my father caught and brought home
to briefly bang the walls of the murky tank of our living room.

A goldfish won at the Burger King parking lot carnival.
We blew too heavy on his gills, cried when he bloated in a teacup.

Gentleman Charlie we abducted while he crossed the street,
technically he was ours if we avoided the missing turtle signs.

A cat my sister named after a popular girl for the pleasure
of saying *I'm going home. Kaitlyn is waiting for me.*

The boy who was dropped at a church where my father was janitor,
skinny boy with the look of a deer about to bolt. My mother told us

not to ask why someone had put nail polish on his small fingers.
We kept quiet when she served him meat on macaroni night.

The guy on the motorcycle that crashed near our hedges
shaved head, in just a t-shirt in summer. My father grabbed

towels, even the dirty ones, all of them smelling always
of a smoker's house and told us to stay inside, don't look.

TASTING RED

My shortcut to the candy store -
a slide between yards
and chain link escapes -
made it easy to slip from
my door to the Swedish fish jar.

Their sticky bodies
a sugar school
globs of heads and tails
almost opaque ruby
cool dust, dead eye.
A precious weight,
an anonymous haul,
made for my tongue.

I could eat a bag in minutes
swallow until my throat
burned sugar.
I stopped cutting
through the yard

after I hooked my leg
on the fence.
Sliced clean, my kneecap
the small end piece of bread,
blood clotting sand and gravel
of the neighbor's yard.

SOMETHING FRAGILE

The milk at the one-stop
is now $4.49 a gallon, and the best
expiration date is just moments away.
It's riskier to stock something fragile;
there's more money to be made selling
lottery tickets and power balls.
You don't want to believe this
as you go to pay, but know it's true -
the stools off to the side of the cash
register were never about convenience.
They are filled with tired bodies hunched over hopes
and lucky nickels, eyes glazed like donut holes.
You are the lost leader, the democratic vote.
On the radio, you hear a chipper woman from
the new Boston Tea Party say nothing, with the conviction
of a cheerleader who's never had to work hard to win a game,
while you were diligent in primary rules -
maybe skipping your lunch to make it to the polls,
maybe letting your kid slide the ballot
into the machine so that she could feel in charge.
With no corporate spending limit, the senator on the radio
proudly tells you that this is a windfall for the First
Amendment, for the fundamental right to free speech.
You want to call in, to have your two cents,
to explain that his wall of sound has none
of the tenor and timbre of one solitary, fragile voice.
Tell him that a noisy cheer, like "a dollar and a dream,"
never rings true, but you rarely get through
on a call-in show, you've got to get ready to get
to work if you are lucky,
and the milk has already started to turn.

MORNING PARADE
July 4, 2022

We are lined up at the fence like every year
but I notice not all of us take the small flags
and there's an awkward moment when
the flag lady circles back to trumpet the offer again.
Someone comments that the kids on the floats
are throwing the candy with a new assertion,
targeting us with starbursts and sweet tarts.
A stress ball hurled by a girl in braids
is a direct, harmless hit. She smiles.
For a moment, still early on this morning,
I let myself love a slice of America,
a coach who wanted them to throw
hard in this tough season
but not hurt anyone.

URSA MINOR

In Boston a father would rather
a son be a trapper
or better yet a bear.
All claws and growl,
a ferocious boy
playing hockey and mauling.

But you, my first affection,
were less Bruin, more teddy,
scared of the hockey rink
a polar fumble on hard ice.
You were to me a singular star.

A champion sweatshirt
over knuckle paw, nose always cold,
I wanted to give you my gamey girl heat
my leg warmers, my thick winter coat,
feed you with food from trees and picnic baskets.

The waiting for ice time early Saturday mornings
by grizzlies who hibernate in idling pick-ups,
mark their territory, leave a stale scent,
and deny all relation to constellations.

I think of how your father bought you
all that equipment to bulk you up before the season -
suspenders, padded pants, steel blades, a mouth guard, a cup
and sent you out to the frozen tundra, open hunting

for bears who have no knowledge of the wild.
Bears pink and new and scared of other bears.
Bears with the eyes of deer before cars.
Bears whose padded bodies hang on the bones
of a much smaller animal,
raised by Boston fathers, original carnivores,
who yell from the den to toughen their young.

ASKING THE CHILDRENS' HOSPITAL TO CORRECT THEIR ENTRANCE SIGN
Buffalo, New York

A small sickle
misplaced should be
a tickle in the throat.
I could block the blemish
from view but already
I've stopped hearing
ambulances as they circle
and park, stopped seeing through
my kitchen window
the pace of parents,
even Amish in bonnets
who travel with what
they themselves
cannot repair.

I've given my parking spot
to friends, their son's heart
open. I gave the space
to a student the semester
she didn't deliver
any essays
and lost
a baby.
It does not salve,
this incision
in the wrong place
sure as stone.
And I'd like to believe
that here it should matter,
the belonging of one
to the other
in number and degree.

RESOLUTION

Too quiet for noise makers,
I wanted to rub raw all the
mylar shine, pop every balloon
until they too were deflated.

We canceled the New Year's Eve party,
the one we held every year, the one
where someone made elephant ears,
flaky with 365 layers of dough.

Our days had been buttered, good until now.
Our lips were trumpets, our hands streamers.
December 1999, we dressed in purple lace
grinding down the decade to Prince.

Another year, guests were high on the deck.
We worried if the rotted planks could hold
the heavy stomp of our joy.
The giddy slur of *YES* and *US*.

I kissed everyone at midnight in moonlight.
Husbands, neighbors, a couple from up
the street who met in a magic show.
I was a fist bump in a fringe dress.

Those years after the countdowns of kids,
forts were built with blankets in living rooms.
Small socks and champagne corks were
found tucked in the couch sleeping it off.

If you had knocked on our door
even in the March tail of winter,
you would have found confetti, small gold
stars, winking from under the porch.

But last year, no party. How could we

move the broken centerpiece of us to set
party store glasses in a tipsy formation?
We were coupe, flute, a breakable inheritance,

the delicate thing you can't bring out and share,
the resolution before midnight,
the buzzkill, the bare lightbulb
in a poorly painted room of empty coats on beds,
the one that points out all the spots you might have missed.

TEST YOUR STRENGTH

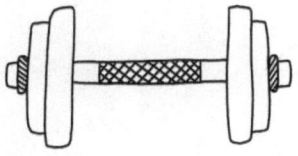

**CAROL ORZEL DONATES HER TWO SKELETONS
TO SCIENCE WITH THE STIPULATION
THAT HER JEWELRY BE DISPLAYED BESIDE THEM**
After the exhibit *Henry and Carol* at the Mütter Museum,
Philadelphia, PA

One misspelled letter in the DNA chain
instructed her soft tissue to turn to bone.

What once might attach, a pandora
charm, now channel set, a setting.

And it kept repeating, stones of a tennis bracelet,
tendon then bone, muscle to bone, bone on bone.

She didn't waste time recounting her rare
inheritance. She built tools. She bought jewelry.

Ribbons and sheets and plates,
it pissed her off that bones seemed

named like dowdy housewares in hope chests.
She'd rather her doubling skeleton be a dowry of bling:

single lady cocktail ring, her ossified left knee,
her collarbone, a pave diamond choker,

a cobra brooch with ruby eyes coiled in her body.
She named her pelvis *Statement Piece*

attached a handle to a vanity mirror to show it off
to herself and the medical students of Philadelphia.

When her ribcage realized it was working
in the service of her F bombs and belly laughter,

it expanded as hard as it could to clear
the imaginary dance floor of her heart and lungs,

which she had come to think of as her cage dancers
in chandelier earrings and tight good jeans.

WHEREBY I AM THE BROKEN WOODEN HEM GUIDE

Again in the dream of sewing notions
and already I hunger to be the silver teeth
of a vintage separating zipper

not this claptrap, a stiff contraption, my body.
I'm sick of biting soundless velvet,
crushing indigo pile, spitting out shantung.

I do want to be a little tougher tonight
more useful than the buttonhole
showy with my stitches done up in silk floss.

In this dream I get tattoos, French
seamed badass tissue paper biceps
designed by an alteration genius
who specializes in pockets and sailcloth.

I sleep like a pin cushion thrown in a drawer
so it cuts across the grain to now be this, broken.
I want the sleep of satin binding fleece,
demand to be a baby on a stuffed red tomato.

In the chase scene, every dream has one,
I drop the small markings of sixteenth inches
from my cranky wooden frame,

drop everything that holds me back.
drop bastings to be redone in new red.
ditch the remnants in a garment district alley.

I dream, I wake, and I work
like a miracle mouth, hinge oiled.
Like a lace maker's hardened thumb.

They'd never imagine me the maker
of something so fine and whose job
is no longer to let something down.

AMERICAN LAUNDRESS RESPONDS TO DEGAS
After the painting *A Woman Ironing* by Edgar Degas

You've left them to believe
how I must quarrel and drink.
Bleaching my toil, and blushing my cheek,
leaving the impression that I've sat for you.

That look is not a coquettish glance.
I'm cataloging the weight of work,
taking inventory of my tools.

The *Flat Iron*, its Vulcan name
dressed in filigree on the stand
is hidden, always hidden,
an indulgence buried at day's end.

The *Sad Iron* is the heaviest.
Its handle becomes that of crutches
warmed wood stained through
with palm oil and pressure.

The *Ruffle Crimper*, a dance hall name,
good for a direct shot into a pleat,
is the iron shaped like a bullet.

THE NEW ENGLAND SMOKESTACK SPEAKS
OF HER DECOMMISSION

Those who knew me, will tell you I was fantastic
at puzzles: hard scrabble, crosswords - great with grids.
I've danced with every mayor. I was a hoofer.
Now as an old lady and dying - there I said it -
I can still tempt a young artist to fire my belly.

In the fifties the boys on the floor
nicknamed me *American Confidence.*
Everyone had a noisy aunt, like me,
who wore stove pipe pants well
showy as a new washing machine, a Cadillac.
Of course I smoked. We all did.

I've had a good run. Stretches of days without injury. 347.
As any broken body knows, one is the heaviest number
to hoist back on the board. How I've come to hunch.
Posture problems, turned my back to breathless neighbors.
Who hasn't dragged soot into a house at one time?

So it goes with powerful women, Grendel's Mother.
Dismantle, defend, I've heard on the harbor wind.
Broad backed, I block the view, a mother at a stove
a shadow in the doorway, a monster under the bed.
I am the desire for light at night. I'm also that light.
We are all incandescent to someone, if briefly.

My four humors - management, union, oil and coal.
It won't be bile to bring me down. And it certainly won't
be my bones - banisters, balconies, church height window -
a ligature of tall, rounded pride.
Shoulders back, back then fuming.

Not too long ago I could pump my legs
and make the water warm, bring barges.
They gossip I blacken fish on the grill, pulverize when I chew

Saying *look at that appetite*. I'll remind them I also cooked
a fine meal in the McIntire District. I was a company picnic,
one hell of a house warming, a light on in every room.

You know only your anatomy so you don't know quite
how to ask. It's a fair question. My lungs? How do I work?
Respirator? Iron cage? Pinball? Like you
my veins run under the city through every small comfort.
Soon my labored breath will stop.
I'll remember that what kept me going,
in and out, swallow or bellow,
was something very much human.

SKIRT

I keep you around solely
for the sound you make.

Gathered at my hips and waist so
much it seems like a family reunion.

Unflattering cut, shallow pocket,
blue, yet gray, a graphite hard on Moleskine.

Unlined. My mother now blind
will soon forget my voice and words

but might remember my body
as a rustle, moving in and out.

AFTER MY MOTHER REFUSES THE RESTRAINING ORDER AGAINST MY FATHER

I go up to their apartment
drop the plastic bags my mother
is bringing home from her rehab
near the couch where we watched movies
when I worked at a video store, good days,
before my dad went off script in technicolor.
Back then, I could take home the new releases
customers didn't rewind. *In medias res:*
Isabella Rossellini naked on the lawn,
Raging Bull on the ropes, Red Rum,
endings that made starting over hard to do.
I ask my mother to tell me
what to do next. *What? What?*
Her only poem, a list of
food to restock the fridge:
paper towels, bread, rotisserie chicken.
I get the cheap, generic brands.
I dent the Wonder - the last soft thing.
My mother taught me *mean* is a silent film star.
My father taught me how to windmill punch.
He is getting a cab voucher from the psych ward,
they hand these out it seems. He gets three days.
Jesus. My father's passion is to get home. My mother never
ate chicken. Lacks the patience for small bone work,
so I know she plans to let him in. Cue the lights.
I leave before this movie ends,
go instead to my friend's poetry class.
He's a good teacher. Each student's
draft rights a picture frame in the apartment,
wipes clean the ash from the kitchen table.
You might want to knock off the last few lines,
he tells his writing students.
Let go of an ending that's not working.

YES, I THINK THAT SHIRT IS PERFECT ON YOU

The hydrangeas on either side of her, just watered,
nodded in formal tribute to the miniature Karl Lagerfeld
in front of them. Their acidic blue heads embarrassed,
as if they were matching gossips just caught, runway
models heavied by the waiting around and eternal bright lights.

I heard the soft earth of invitation in her voice,
noted her sophisticated slicked back hair. A small wet pup.
Silhouette of yet. *Do you like this shirt?* she asked,
posing in our garden on the first day of 7th grade.
I held the camera and cropped those thirsty blooms.

The shirt was cotton with cuffs and a collar, sure of itself,
as if planting a foot and ready to roll a sleeve.

I would have named her *White Amaryllis in the Dead of Winter*
had it been an offering in the seed packet of baby names,
had I known of her hardiness or could have forecasted such a bloom.

JET BOAT STYLE

During swimming lessons
at the Sterling Center YMCA,
I pitch forward on the
aluminum bleacher to witness
the semi-finals of scoop paddle,
the nationals of floating.

Her shoulder straps ride side saddle
and her hair sasses me back already.
Still, now, it is impossible for her
to be an *A & P* queen, a bathing-suit girl
because my daughter is five.

Mrs. Seal hands out noodles,
clicks hunchback bubbles, and
kids carbonate that water while she barks out metaphors:
Butterfly arms, Cannonball, legs like scissors.
My girl tells me *My hair is jet boat style, Mama.*
Thick as waves.

Sometimes she scrawls comment cards
because she knows what she needs.
Growling desires – more bubbles
longer shower, corn muffins at snack bar-
like an inmate with a list of demands if she
is to endure her small container.

In the locker room, the manatees from the ten o'clock
water aerobics crackle complaints of cold water,
dusting their underpants with powder,
standing on non-skid soles.
But a five-year-old can't get cold,
a motor-boat motor-boat circulates just under the skin.

You go girl. Defy that timed shower,
hit the button again to fill your small suit.

Keep working to trap the water between fabric and skin, teaching a body to puff out proud.

KNOCKDOWN

From this corner, the moss-marked fence gives the toothless grin
of a sucker taking blows from branches. Root and post wrestle
underground, a bare-knuckle history that goes deep.

The great American elm always shadowed Palooka Fence,
who won't answer to Dutch, who has memorized
the grace of butterflies, who felt the haymaker punch of '78,

both opponents scarred with pulleys from Depression-time
clotheslines. For the elm, it's an enswell embedded,
a knot in this contender's eye that always stares down pride.

When the knockdown happens—a flash storm
no one saw coming—phantom limbs scratch the eyes
of the house and spit small seeds into a now fenceless yard.

ILLUSION SHOW

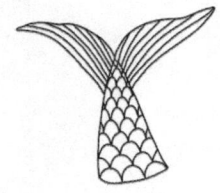

SOLSTICE

After we've oohed to the bald-headed moon
after the fire has snapped a backyard lilac
and sparklers are a fizzle of tails swimming down the sidewalk,
someone moons over Iceland, a solstice to eclipse this block party.

On Coney Island, the mermaids are hauling their parade tails
from closets, pulling the packing tape from cardboard boxes
where they have stowed away their iridescence,
their crescent moon spandex scales and mussel shell bras.
It is worth the effort. It is only once a year.

NANCY DREW AND THE CASE OF THE MYSTERIOUS WILL

You ditched the plastic pumpkin
for a smart burnished satchel, a clue
to your pragmatic need for candy
on a night of gorging and bobbing
and greedy masked faces of boys.

We made your blue dress together.
I spy you taking notes about collars of the era.
Premeditated, you cut your hair in early October.
You would have dyed it blonde and pin curled
each lock, if you had agency beyond third grade.

You have no use for the Spooky Store, kitten ears
or princess veils. What you want is a clock,
old and German, or skeleton key with heavy
filigree, hidden in a hedge on Halloween.

There will be no dayglow bones or blinking safety wand.
You will coast up a driveway in a blue roadster
to the obvious house, the one with the full-size
candy bars and useful pencils, orange and black.

Carry that clock under your arm. Interrogate every knight
by Titian porch light. *What is your quest?*
You will spiral an apple peel until the mystery is solved,
brilliant and genuine as the pearls at your neck.

WE ARE ALL SMALL BOATS FLOATING INWARD

As fragile as it seems,
make the boat of paper.
You know it might be done for,
up against more than you can imagine.
But go ahead - origami, birch bark canoe -
crease as suits the cut of your jib.
Send it out on one agreeable bobbing wave.
Give it to the spitting wind in storm season.
Turn away or look. But return quickly,
before lightening lowers the boom
or charges the scene in flattering light,
back through scrub pine, back home,
back to where you build your small craft.

ARS POETICA

One student carries a foam sword
orientates a cape towards wind
always they are fighting some dragon
distracting the ring-nosed bull with red.

Sometimes I see them in the consignment shop
searching for the swashbuckling section
of which, of course, there is and there isn't. I imagine
they begin every day in chant: *Once upon a time*
perchance, me thinks puffed up words
billowing at the throat, stories told as scarf dance.

I wouldn't flinch if they came to class with a walking stick
so many of us with props that say look over there,
pay no attention to the shark cage I'm wearing.

And then this student writes a poem, a first
I believe. Each line carries the weight of dropped armor.
No twist of a waxed mustache, which they are not opposed
to wearing. No girl left on the tracks.

In an office without character
we sit together with the poem
until it has buried a father,
in Georgia on a hot day, no fanfare,
just the exquisite buzz in the first line

then gnats circling back in a perfect turn to distract
the mourners who have brought food to the house.

AFTER THE SURGEON DRAWS ON MY LEG WITH A SHARPIE

my art student shows me her new tattoo.
She doesn't know I've been told I will need
a knee replacement, and maybe a hip.

It's a skull, dead center, there on her thigh.
My knee, a boxer's fist inside a glove,
swells against her youth, this too-close treasure

mapping her future story on the skin.
Her bone face is an outline yet to be filled.
When she has time, maybe on break, she says.

She has pulled the metal out of her ears
replaced the posts with scorpion spacers
entombed in amber, ancient and dead.

I don't tell her, but, if I got gages
I'd want fresh babies, ear loafs, something young
and doughy to show for all that stretching.

Like the Bosch she has planned for her forearm,
the little neck stars will be inked in, in time.
She says this as if the stars were infinite.

THE SNOW EXPLAINS ITS FALLING TO YOU

Because I could see your incantation as breath on the solarium pane. I heard the pen across white-lined paper as morning vespers, summoned. Because I want you to have some inheritance. It is hard to look up, in these abscess tooth days, this floor of sawdust, our shuffle and squall never melting together as a deep, clear reservoir. Because I am called a scattering, a dusting, Nor'easter, a blanket, a front, a force. I am offering you dance steps for silent pond ice, my choreography for disappearing acts desperate to stay. Because cold and desolate are the accumulating version of my story as told by the stranded in an airport terminal. I'm asking you to take me in at the back of your collar as an exclamation and speak my name like a child would. I am a collective noun. I am a congress. And I will fall as I will fall.

REVERSIBLE DRESS: AN APOLOGY

I thought I could repair it
this bias shift, white as a flag. Waving
a pattern passed down, fitting
me no more. *Why don't you?*
Ease is just a fabrication
based on cutting lines.
I worried through my needle's eye
the false and blind stitches and hemming.
I'm sure everyone could see
you. Like a fool
I practiced altering
to make a better fit
before I knew
how to mend a dress for a child.

How to mend? Address for a child:
Before I knew
to make a better fit
I practiced altering
you, like a fool.
I'm sure everyone could see
the false and blind - stitches and hemming -
I worried through my eyes. *Needle*
me no more why don't you?
Based on cutting lines,
ease is just a fabrication,
a pattern passed down fitting
this bias. Shift. White as a flag waving:
I thought I could repair it.

BARBARA WAS KNOWN TO POOL HOP

I tell her she must cross the meal and mush, a curse upon Galileo,

this crab apple pile in the corner of a cousin's yard.

Climb the swing set, its steady hiccup of pole leaving ground,

its slack jaw chain, now quiet at night. Convince my accomplice.

Curse the wood chips, the suburbs, other people's pools.

A whirlpool is the push back, a powerful crave, made

by moving in circles. That's the most energy Barbara

would allow after sliding into the pool past midnight.

Her hair a permanent defiance which she would not get wet,

could not relax, and so we kept our movements too small,

shoulders above the water, canceling out our audacity.

Her hair glistened with droplets, small worlds,

each anticipating the fall to come.

HOUSE OF VOICES

one is an inconsolable

    owl hoot of *Who cooks for you?*

        I do, I do, a clavicle craned, turning back

another in the shower saves all

    singing and excitable words for water

        washing full vowels down the drain

one talks in only equations, subsists on the

    sugar of pie charts and a math of unequal parts

        If you get this, then I get more

there's a gossip around here too

    sometimes hospitalized for mouth sores

        a saint holding bees in her mouth

    an orator in front of an open fridge, singing

cold arias for clementines and spoiled meat

hands held open like shovels

offering cake

a short story reader we all call the liar,

the one who collects Polaroids and talks only of memory

the whisperer with cattails for tonsils

WINNER, WINNER, CHICKEN DINNER

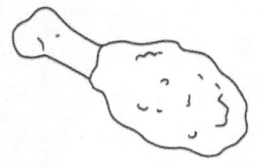

THE LAST BATH OF THE FIRST SNOW
for E.L.M.

This might be the last bath we will take
together, so of course I say yes
after shoveling and traveling
from your north to south pole,
a trudge between the mounds
made from the porch to the car.

Anyway, if I keep you out any longer
you'll get too cold and we might dig too deep,
reveal the grit of gravel that embarrasses
our perfect journey like something caught
in between a tooth. A spoiler.

We leave the snow to its clean perfection,
let nature and traffic be the ones to muck it up.
It won't always be this smooth,
so we take that bath.

The house is warm
the door so strong between climates.
We take off all our layers
and there are many
probably more than you need.

In the hallway I ask you to stay
near me and that's all you know you do.
We unroll our cuffs and let the matted
snow, pats of chilled butter, give up on the carpet.

Your pants are a thick wet
under that your PJ's are sopped too.
Your little red thighs cold to the touch.

You delight in the red tinge of my skin,
knowing that you are of me.

We run up the stairs in just our undies
and you love this part, think it's better than toast.
You ask if we can hold hands. Of course, we can hold hands.
We laugh as we try to fit our cold compressed
bodies on the same bare step
your happiness is in your mouth,
the way all your square first teeth line up.

Do you know too
that this might be the last time
with me in the bath?

We sing about riding in the car. I'm the driver.
I suspect you give this one to me.
Our knees sink under the water. A tight fit,
our different displacements.

You don't reach out for me with your baby need,
but you let me mother you. I wash your hair
letting the water
swerve around your perfect ear
as if you are snow
that I don't want to melt.

HOW TO MAKE MOZZARELLA

It is best to be in love, in the company of love,
or at the very least aware that love binds.

Untangle some knot, plant a garden from seed.
Do not give up, even if it's September with tomatoes

still green. There are paper bags full of our kind
and Honeycrisp to rally us into the better season.

Don't be put off by the necessary sour.
It's no more complicated than a good joke -

the kind that startles you by how well it worked.
It's the starter, the kiss at the door, a quick chemistry.

Don't sweat which pot or what milk.
Everything is reactive or nonreactive.

Dinner comes down to how you tell a story.
The guest who worried for the cheese,

cheered when it was salty and smooth,
indeed cheese, brings her best to our dining room.

On the day the phonebooks were delivered, she opens.
See how you can go anywhere with a line like that?

We could name the cows when dinner was over.
Our bellies were drums, our basil confetti.

A cardigan slumped on the kitchen chair
I didn't know until that night, that all cheese begins

as mozzarella, a humble gathering at the top of the pot,
caves of flavor, sweet or pungent, of our making.

RACE POINT AFTER ILLNESS
Provincetown, Massachusetts

We hear peepers under the porch
and high five, toast their evening chorus.
We've been told what droughts can do
how some seasons the tadpoles
won't get the time to grow legs,
make it to marsh get on with it.
We are here, in a rented room
of a protected lighthouse,
to get on with it.
Here, where tide turns ampersand.

We have just abandoned our roadside attraction
putt-putt golf. The sign *Use All Things at Your Own Risk*
makes a burden of which pencil, club or ice cream cone.
All new risks on artificial grass, all wrong things.
We leave before the last hole takes the ball for good
leave it in play for someone else and get out quick.

The windsock windmills hello or goodbye
along Route 6 then drop its ribbon arms.
I hold a new sadness for stillness before storms
curse the wind for not being more direct with us
and skywriting, *I can knock the purpose
out of you just by playing dead.*

We follow the path of snakes through dunes
curve around shacks of drifters to the lighthouse
who tells us half a story:

You've heard it only takes a few feet.
Good swimmers still get lost at sea.
In a summer of seals, soft heads bobbing,
it is possible to see a shark if you want to.
Everything will seem fin and teeth forever.

Decide right now what you will see.

INTENSIVE CARE CONVERSATION

If you *had* died, you say,
imagine the casseroles!
I would have had
to run out to Best Buy
to purchase a freezer
for the basement
and more forks
for those late night
pickings under foil,
toasted and buttered
breadcrumbs made
by Italian women
from your book club,
pot pies from PTA moms.

There is no hot dish
that will comfort
you, I say,
our basement is
haunted
with photographs,
remember.
I plan to bend all
the tines in the drawer.
Already the salt
is hidden, my love.
Whenever you took
a bite, something would
have been missing.

AT THE TAPAS RESTAURANT, TWO TABLES OF GIRLFRIENDS EACH PERFORMING SCENES FROM *SEX IN THE CITY*

When the plates start arriving
we allow the fiddleheads their modesty,
curled in tight like most green spring things.
They've turned their backs to us like freshman girls
who know the trick of taking off a bra
without showing anything.

We are seasoned enough to find them charming,
not put off by these new fresh belly buttons,
and we hold back on salting our tender skins.

When the table next to us orders cava
we encourage them in their bravado.
They are celebrating. The prettiest one,
and they are all pretty, has turned twenty-eight.
Opening wide they position their throats under the porron
like hungry birds waiting for mothers to feed them.

We are tender enough to find them charming,
not put off by these new fresh belly buttons,
and we hold back on salting our seasoned skins.

WHEN THE BOOKMOBILE LADY DRIVES DOWN YOUR STREET

When the bookmobile lady drives down your street
consider her to be behind the controls of an invisible plane.
Sharpen your sight and shout Shazam!
Don't fall for the glasses on the chain thing.
It's an insider joke, mostly for show.
She's got 20/20, heat seeking vision, a third eye.

Under the cuffs of her cardigan she wears
the steel bracelets of Wonder Woman.
You want to ban a gay penguin, try it lady.
She'll march you up to the third floor of the library
to the justice league, the federation of free thought
and politely, yet firmly, remind you of the little matter
of civil liberty. She keeps the lasso of truth in her belt loop.

I've seen the jokers who try to trip up the reference librarians.
Riddle me this, Reference Librarian,
When was the Great Vowel Shift?
I need a romantic, but not cheesy, poem for a wedding
and I don't want any capital letters in it.
How do I get the garlic smell off my hands?
Feathers unruffled she hands them a piece of scrap paper,
wasting little lead on her miniature golf pencil:
15th-18th *centuries. Try ee cummings. Vinegar.*
Touché, librarian, touché.

Once a librarian was asked to switch careers,
pull a Freaky Friday with an archenemy.
A Lex Luthor - *A Vegas Showgirl.*
Well, it seems that the librarian with her large
head full of information and strong sense of balance
had no problem supporting the feathered headgear.
So skilled she was at entering other worlds by cracking spines
that you couldn't pick her out of the high-kicking lineup.
The showgirl, for all her staged glitter and flesh tone,
was only useful as a page. Stacked, but only able to shelve.

If you rush to return a book at 10 to 9, pay attention
to this twilight time between mortal and divine,
those of us who borrow and those who freely lend.
The librarians are putting on their magnificent wings
and gorgeous shoes, stepping out of phone booths,
setting up a buffet near the microfilm.

FOR THE BUYER OF BREAKFASTS IN SALEM

I wish for you a lifetime of eggs
over easy, poached, sunny side up
on a raft, scrambled with Vermont cheddar.

I wish for you that every time you walk
into the diner on Washington St.
somebody says, *What do ya know, Jo.*

You're that guy, the one who secretly
shelled out to strangers. Just 'cause.
Hot ticket. Mayor of the counter.

I wish for you that when the story gets
English muffin dry and day-old stale
you will still be known as lumberjack.

Pass him the sports page, pass him the syrup,
give him a warm up, little creamers on ice.
No, bring him the real milk from the cooler.

Every small generosity is now yours to pocket:
parcels and postcards, secret santas,
the resurrection of men's hat departments.

All those hats worn by other nice men
who will search for you on sidewalks
just for the chance to tip a brim in your direction.

I wish for you full satisfaction:
not from the silver-dollar pancakes -
which are on the house at my thank-you counter -

but because later, when I took your cue
and bought dessert for the couple two tables over,
it tasted sweeter than cannoli.

SNAPDRAGON, BACHELOR BUTTON, SWEET PEA

One summer we neglected to deadhead,
by winter our favorite flowers were still around,
vibrant purple and red cuttings that shocked the gray
of cold kitchen counters. They were a hoot.
A grandfather, who had been buried under
at least twenty Irish knit layers of snow,
came back warm blooded.
He draped his russet cardigan,
cuffs worn by tinker fingers,
onto the chiffon shoulders
of your Aunt Millie who arrived
in her 1952 full bloom,
holding a Manhattan glass etched
with tipsy faces made mostly of eyelashes.

Arriving in clusters - snapdragon, bachelor button,
sweet pea - all we had lost, came back heady.
Scooch, I said, for the brittle small stems
of children who never were. Find a spot by the windowsill
for the newly dead still aching to open towards the sun.
Let the angered and the fidgety ghosts
sit by the warming oven. Add rose water to the lemonade.
That winter we made a hothouse of memory,
added aspirin to every cutting.
Later we all rolled up our sleeves and canned
the sour rhubarb into something sweeter.

ONE DAY WE WERE FULL AND FLUSH

I drape my bathing suit over the porch railing right near a mailbox now empty of worry, take out the haddock that had been intended for a school night dinner. I let it swim in olive oil and sweet paprika. I slice garlic while my hair is wrapped in a towel. Squint and I'm an album cover.

Our kid doesn't even care that we are cooking disgusting fish in our underwear totally embarrassing her and *not* getting Chipotle from the mall. She has a new iPhone. We cheated death yesterday, not killing each other at AT&T. Right now, all she knows is that her parents are gross but love each other, love her, and will come to love her iPhone.

We drink wine in short glasses. We take the fish, blistered and red, out to the table. We sit under the purple vine that we did nothing to make beautiful. It just grew beautiful. We stuff our mouths with olives, and you'd swear we were having lunch in the Azores.

We half expect Anthony Bourdain to show up and kick back with us. Compliment my husband on his hairy chest of bread crumbs, proclaim, *This is how you live!* He'd kiss my cheeks and leave paprika stains. He'd even text something to our kid from his identical new iPhone, something like *Tough life, Kid.* And she'd get his sarcasm and respond with an emoji that signified, *I know, I love them too.*

ACKNOWLEDGMENTS

I am grateful to the editors and readers of the following journals and anthologies in which poems in this collection have first appeared or are forthcoming, some in different versions:

Barrelhouse: "When the Bookmobile Lady Drives Down Your Street"

Cider Press Review: "Grand Mall, Pall Mall, Pell-Mell," "In Praise of Swimming at Night"

Cleaning Up the Glitter: "Nancy Drew and the Case of the Mysterious Will"

Clinch: "Knockdown"

Constellations: "Hand to Mouth," "Ursa Minor"

Eastern Iowa Review: "The Snow Explains Its Falling to You"

Eat this Poem: "For the Buyer of Breakfasts in Salem"

Glowworm-Propriception: "The More Weighted the Purse"

Grand Little Things: "The New England Smokestack Speaks of Her Decommission"

Ilanot Review: "Snapdragon, Bachelor Button, Sweet Pea"

Literary Mama: "The Last Bath of the First Snow"

Meat for Tea: "After the Surgeon Draws on My Leg with a Sharpie"

Molecule: "Jury Duty, January"

Mom Egg Review: "Jet Boat Style," "Unmentionables"

Nixes Mate: "Hunger is a Suit Like Farrah's," "Rescues"

Passages North: "Whereby I Am the Broken Wooden Hem Guide"

Paterson Literary Review: "After My Father Refuses the Restraining Order Against My Father," "Blueberry Donuts," "Conflict Resolution Through Soup," "Fried Dough Trailer," "Getting and Spending on Commercial Street," "If You Can't Find God in the Details," "One Day We Were Full and Flush," "Resolution," "Tasting Red"

PoetryMagazine.Com: "Honorable Mention"

Roar: "When All It Took Was Mustard"

Soul Lit: "Magical Thinking"

Up the Staircase Quarterly: "It Is Elizabeth Bishop's Fish"

Vermont Literary Review: "Something Fragile"

———

"Apricots in Afghanistan" and "At the Tapas Restaurant…" appear in *Heroic Care: 35 Writers & Artists Show What It Means to Care*, Ed. Betsy Ellor (Words Unbound, 2021)

"Hand to Mouth" was reprinted in *Raising Lilly Ledbetter: Women Poets Occupy the Workspace*, Eds. Wright, Toledo and Lyons (Lost Horse Press, 2015).

"Conflict Resolution Through Soup" and "Last Bath of the First Snow" were featured in 2016 for the *Compassion Anthology* (Compassionanthology.com)

"The Pea Defends Its Position" was first published in *Modern Grimmoire: Contemporary Fairy Tales, Fables & Folklore*, Ed. Michael Harris Cohen (Indigo Ink Press, 2013).

———

"American Laundress Responds to Degas" appeared originally in 2012 as part of *Artifact, Archive, Orchard*, a poetry collaboration between Montserrat College of Art and the Peabody Historical Society.

"Maggots and Milk" appeared in *Poetry Storehouse* and was re-mixed into film by artist Adriane Little (2016) and was screened at the Motion Pictures International Film Festival (2018).

"We Are All Small Boats Floating Inward" was part of *Line Break*, a commissioned poetry installation at the Peabody Essex Museum in collaboration with artist Lillian P. H. Kology for the Massachusetts Poetry Festival (2016).

"Skirt" and "Yes, I Think that Shirt is Perfect on You" were featured along with handmade clothing for the exhibition, *Shifts*, Montserrat College of Art (2021).

––––––

With many thanks to my Montserrat students and colleagues - I hit the jackpot getting to be in a community of such talented and caring artists. A special thanks to Small Bites Press/Table for Seven, and Erin Dionne who deserves a silk top hat for the magic she summoned to get this book to publication. I am grateful to Kathi Aguero, M.P. Carver, Lis Weiss Horowitz, Jennifer Jean, Kali Lightfoot, Jennifer Martelli, Dawn Paul, and JD Scrimgeour for their advice and encouragement as many of these poems came into being. I'm especially grateful to Kevin Carey, January Gill O'Neil, and Cindy Veach for their puns, spit takes, and small chocolate hearts (respectively) while closely reading and rereading this collection. To the poets, artists, and enthusiastic listeners of the Improbable Places Poetry Tour, you are the giant stuffed bear at the fair, the big prize. Maria Mazziotti Gillan and Susan Rich are poets of the finest order, literary citizens, and the best carnival barkers. To my North Shore family, my Buffalo "momleagues" and mentors, and my Whitehorse ladies: I love you like I love a mod dress, a dance party, a killer grilled cheese. Sue and Dick Michaels, you have made so much possible and joyous for me. Thank you.

Eliza, you are beyond remarkable and better than any poem I could ever write. I love you.

Chris, you are the groove in my heart, my love supreme.

ABOUT THE AUTHOR

Colleen Michaels was born in Waltham, Massachusetts and graduated from the University of Buffalo and the State University of New York - Fredonia. Her poetry has been published widely, anthologized, and made into public installations for the Trustees of Reservations and the Massachusetts Poetry Festival. She serves on the board of trustees for the Beverly Public Library, is the creator of the Improbable Places Poetry Tour, and directs the Writing Studio at Montserrat College of Art in Beverly, Massachusetts, where she lives with her family. *Prize Wheel* is her first collection. You can find her online at colleenmichaels.com

www.ingramcontent.com/pod-product-compliance
Lightning Source LLC
Chambersburg PA
CBHW020329130626
46549CB00003B/1085